Dear Diana: Travel With Me to
Tallinn, Estonia

By Margaret C. Collier
Illustrated by Mary T. Cook

To order additional copies of this book, contact:
Xlibris
1-888-795-4274
www.Xlibris.com
Orders@Xlibris.com

This book is dedicated to my friends in Estonia, particularly Diana, who is attending the University and making her dreams come true with the support of her mother, Vica and her grandparents who are in the now Russian sector of Crimea.

It is also dedicated to the steadfast help of family and to my friend, Mary T. Cook.

# Tallinn, Estonia

This collage represents some of my favorite memories of my recent visit to Tallinn, Estonia. The pictures show us a beautiful city that embodies our modern times as well as the medieval buildings that once made it a very important center of trade and culture in the 14th, 15th and 16th centuries.

Tallinn is a designated UNESCO heritage site. It was a city that contained thriving guilds of trade and beautiful churches that contained many works of priceless art and the presentation of a way of life making Tallinn a very prosperous city at one point in the older European history annals. It is today a beautiful city that is independent and it embraces the technologies of our modern world which aid in the showcasing of marvelous examples of a way of life found only during the medieval history period of northern Europe.

Where is Tallinn, Estonia? Tallinn is located in Northern Europe on the Baltic Sea. It is across the sea from Finland and their capital city of Helsinki. Until 1991 it had been a Soviet satellite country under the auspices of the Soviet Union. Today it is an independent nation modernized by embracing all types of technologies and working hard to maintain a democracy for its citizens. Within Tallinn is the old Medieval City restored and delighting visitors every day, all year long.

Tallinn, Estonia is a delightful surprise for any traveler. It is a beautiful city in a small country with a great history influenced by the many cultures that have been crossing through its borders over the centuries. The city itself is diversified with modern businesses, restaurants, shops, and many historical areas amidst change and restoration. At its heart is the old city of Tallinn, restored in most of its major areas and attracting many world tourists. The Baltic Sea beckons us to visit Finland and the scenery is beautiful from many vantage points.

Below is a view of the Gulf of Finland.

There is a gorgeous children's park here and the scenic view is breathtaking. Note the blue skies with crystalline white clouds, the air is so wonderfully clean it is a pleasure to just stand and look at the picturesque scenery.

Tallinn has a modern bus and transportation system, making it easy to get around. Walking is always great, easy to do. On the bus I usually encountered many who spoke English, it is taught in the schools and it is a positive for their tourism boom since more and more come from the United States and England. I felt very much at home and very safe. Menus included the English language as did signs in the shops and other shopping areas in the malls that are found all around the city. Signs explaining historical areas are also done in English.

In this small shop near an entranceway to the old city area, I met a couple from Philadelphia buying local jewelry. Like many shops these are original buildings restored and just delightful to go into, transporting you back hundreds of years in your imagination!! Notice the table and chairs, with the small covered table to the right of the store picture. These were outside a coffee shop.

Many shops still maintain a door that displays information about the type of merchandise that they display. The doors are hand carved and are closer to being works of art rather than just a plain door. Some have doll displays by the entryways; others have a small sign for display carved in the shape of the merchandise that is sold. Below is a sign over an old wine shop.

This door on page 5 depicts the Blackhead Guild that successfully operated in Old Tallinn at the height of its success. The carving and the fine use of color and texture draws the customers' eyes in immediately.

Many of the streets are still paved inside the medieval city in cobblestone fashion giving you a good idea of how it would be to walk on roadways versus the even paved streets in the modern parts of the city. I loved every alleyway since the streets really lend themselves to the atmosphere.

Also common are the red tiled roofs which have been restored. Stores such as Old Hansa seen above sell a variety of goods such as you might have found centuries ago. Their meal menu includes several recipes using the reindeer as a principle meat. Small plays and skits along with music often are the entertainment during the colder months just as they were in centuries gone past.

During the tsarist rule in Russia, Estonian lands were under Russian rule. Prior to the Russians, Germany and Sweden had occupied the lands currently known as Estonia. Germany conquered the area in the late 1200's and ruled for four centuries, then the Swedish invaded and while they were progressive, Russia became involved because German landowners asked for Russian help to maintain their estates. By 1709 the Russians were in firm control of the land. It was not until the 1917 revolution and over throw of czarist rule that Estonia began to consider that it could be independent once again. The end of World War II saw Estonia once more under Russian influence and it was not until the late 1980's that Estonia was able to revitalize their culture and small businesses. When the USSR collapsed in 1991, they were somewhat prepared for the independence that came overnight.

Kadriorg palace below is a reminder of the highly opulent era of Czar Peter the Great.

The grounds of the palace are best appreciated in the spring and summer with its plethora of flowers and flowering trees and bushes. The gardens are unique in their design and the grounds are cared for on a year round basis. My friends in Tallinn feel fall is the best time to see the estate due to the myriad of colors from the different species of deciduous trees.

The palace is filled with beautiful works of art and the ceilings are done in baroque style, reminiscent of Old Italian villas and the architecture of which Peter the Great was very fond. Even the furniture that is on display projects the richness in which the palace was designed and furnished. The original cottage that Peter the Great and his wife spent early summers in has been turned into a small museum on the grounds of the estate, often used for field trips by local school children.

This look at the interior on page 10 offers a better view of the ornate architecture.

The beauty and opulence give us a good idea of expectations for dwellings in the day of Peter the Great. It is not difficult to conjure up images of wonderful house parties and elegant guests. Even the doll's corner is enchanting!

Peter the Great

Peter the Great was an imposing figure. This portrait was painted in 1838 and during his time as the leader of Russia the country amassed great political power.

This stove is a good example of the comforts that were provided in the palace and to the right are tiles showing you the details from the delft blue ceramic style of the Netherlands. There were several of these stoves placed strategically through the palace on both floors as well as some traditional fireplaces. Many servants were maintained to keep the palace up to standards of expectation on a year round basis even though it was primarily considered a summer residence. Other wealthy nobles also had estates in Tallinn as well as other European countries. Furniture such as the couch below was also known for its elegance.

In addition to the beautiful summer palace Tallinn is also known for its elegant churches and the art contained in them as well as their architecture.

The architecture of this impressive church, Alexander Nevsky's Cathedral, was not welcome by the citizens of Talinn during its construction. It was too much a reminder of the oppression that the Estonians felt at the hands of the Russians. The oniontop domes, with the crosses of gold, were opulent and inside the church, the altarpieces were also very extravagant. It was constructed during the czarist rule of Alexander III and it was believed to have been built over the gravesite of a beloved Estonian folk hero, Kalev.

This beautiful view of Tallinn from the Patkuli viewing platform gives you a good view of the old red tiled roofs and also the spires of city churches. One of the tallest spire seen is that of the Cathedral of St. Mary the Virgin, built in 1240 AD. It is the oldest church maintaned in Estonia, mostly built of wood. It is a very important church and represents the heart of worship for Estonian Lutherans. The spire seen in the forefront belongs to St. Olav's Church built in the 14th century.

Another very important church is that of the Niguliste Church. It contains many beautiful altarpieces and hand carved statuary. There is also a chamber housing silver from the early guild known as the Brotherhood of the Blackheads.

During World War II the church sustained bombing damages but was restored as soon as possible once the conflict ended. The church holds regular services and houses artwork which make it a museum as much as a church.

Walking through the church is a feast for the eyes as you view beautiful paintings, altarpieces and wood carvings overlayed in gold leaf. It is an ongoing site of restoration and preservation.

The inside with wooden pews and beautiful stained glasses windows. The building itself is a work of art. The large altarpiece, which is about the death of Saint Nicholas, was painted in 1482 by the German artsit Hermen Rode of Lubeck, Germany. This altarpiece shows a vairiety of scenes from the life of Saint Nicholas.

A panel from The Danse Macabre is seen below.

The Danse Macabre is the church's most treasured piece of artwork. This frieze depicts death dancing with the kings and nobles, enticing them to join death. Painted in the late 1400's its meaning is open to interpretation and considering the fact that the medieval times were ending and the Renaissance was approaching, it is an indication of changing times.Others feel that the message contained within was that death comes to all of us, poor or rich, noble or peasant.

The Church of St. Nicholas also contsined many wood carved features on its walls. The carvings often depict the coats of arms of patron families. Below is an orginal confessional still used today at mass.

In addition to the beautiful churches many shops often have small, intimate museums. Along the cobble stone streets, I found a marzipan shop housing one such museum with beautiful examples of sculptures done with marzipan, a type of candy. We have animals, a wedding cake and a doll below.

The creation of such materpieces is a time honored tradition and requires infinite patience!! It tasted pretty good also, we were given free samples of this traditional candy.

The largest and roundest tower from the old city is affectionately known as "Fat Margaret". With walls that are about 4 feet thick, it has been transformed into the Estonian Museum of Maritime History. Below you can see the windows used for defense with cannon. The tower seen on page 19 is attached to other buildings here at the gateway to the city from the Baltic Sea.

The museum houses a variety of artifacts that are from many types of boats and periods of naval history, going back to the days of the Viking influence and up to and through World War II and modern naval history. The sea has always been a large part of Estonia's economy and its history. The top floor of the museum gives you several beautiful views of the land and sea surrounding Tallinn.

The tower served as a prison at one point but cease to be that after the uprising against Russia's czar in 1917.

The museum also depicts examples of sea life (top photo) with a fanciful look at the many places the ships from Estonia have sailed .There is a model of a beautiful multi-masted ship used in the 18th and 19th centuries.

Taking a stroll through the streets of Old Tallinn you can certainly get a feel for the standard of living that once existed centuries ago at the zenith of Tallinn's success. You can almost close your eyes, and see how people probably bustled through the streets going about their daily routines of business.

Above are some scenes of the lovely streets and old buildings in Tallinn. The lower left corner shows an alleyway leading into the old city. Note the top left picture, what piece of modern technology do you see? The upper right shows me outside of the Old Hansa Inn with a menu posted below much it might have been centuries ago.

European countries are noted for their unique Christmas markets and their "old world" atmosphere for this lovely holiday and its emphasis on natural greenery and light. Tallinn uses the beauty of the old medieval setting in the town square.

Small carved ducks and snails can be found around the squares such as you see in the upper left hand corner. The emphasis on medieval menus and merchandise for sale are promoted as you see in the upper right hand corner. The lower left are beautiful hand made dishes depicting the importance of the horse in Estonia's culture. The Wine Library is in the lower right. You can enjoy wine and read in this lovely old building, a fore runner to our our wine galleries and coffee shops.Below is a typical cobblestone street.

Outside of the downtown Tallinn area is a beautiful and very unusual museum. It is called the Kumu Art Museum. It is unique in its architecture and it houses a beautiful collection of Estonian art as well as many other exhibits. This an aerial view.

The two lower pictures were taken in the courtyard area as you entering Kumu. The structure is built into a limestone bank on the edge of Kadriorg Park.

VISVALDIS ZIEDIŅŠ

The museum houses sculptures such as the "Talking Busts" of famous people and characters in our society (found in the upper left handcorner), as well as oils, acrylics, photo media and a vaiety of different sculptural events. The talking busts are very unique as you can hear each character give a synopsis of themselves and their importance from famous people to cartoon characters such as Bart Simpson.

Much of the artwork is by Estonian artists as well from surrounding Baltic countries. The variety is interesting as you look from gallery to gallery and see tradtional art and more modern interpretations. On the next page are more examples of the art. I really enjoyed in this beautiful museum.

Traditional interpretation of the landscaping in Estonia is tempered with the modern sculpture in the lower right hand corner and the interpretation of Lenin in the lower left hand corner. In the more modern exhibits the use of recycled materials is a frequent medium. In talking to the curator they encourage school trips and they have exhibits from time to time of local artwork from their schools.

In keeping with the use of modern technology Tallinn is the site of a very modern University. Diana, for whom this series of books is named, is very fortunate to attend the Tallinn University of Technology. Estonia is a small country but it has nearly total wifi available everywhere and one of the world's highest mobile phone usage rates. The University reflects its astounding progress since 1991 when it became independent. It is the only school of its type in Estonia.

Inside the University of Technology are spacious areas for study and a library that is as up to date as possible. The outside of the building is covered in a unique building material that allows one to see out but blocks the suns glare while allowing use of its warmth and light.

The University supports several schools of study and it is international in its scope with students from not only Europe but Asia and North America.Nineteen international degree programs exist on their campus. Sixty countries are currently represented by the University and it partners with over 40 universities ( as of 2010) from all over the world.The programs offer Bachelor's Degrees, Masters Degrees as well as some areas for PhD's.

The mascot of Tallinn University of technology is Juulius, "the eternal student." He is representative of the idea that we are all students forever, learning everyday. There is a statue in the courtyard,as seen below, to remind everyone of that idea.There are many different activities in which students can participte as the bulletin board below announces. Note the bottom picture showing you the outside of the library building.

One of the advantages of visiting Tallinn is the ability to catch a Viking cruiseline to Norway, Sweden or Finland for extended visits or day trips. The most convenient day trip is to Helsinki,Finland which is about a 2 hour journey across the beautiful waters of the Baltic.

Helsinki is a bustling, modern city the site of a great deal of history but the home of modern shops and businesses. The Viking cruise lines and ferry boats make it easy for people to travel back and forth. The cruise ship carried people and visitors by car and bus. The beautiful waters of the Baltic were just as blue as the clear sky, being on deck was refreshingly cold!!

The dockside market was a treasure of handmade crafts, a shoppers delight.

Wandering through Helsinki ,we were treated to a number of small restaurants and coffee and pastry shops and since it was Saturday, families were out doing their weekly shopping.The bakery shop below is one of Helsinki's most popular.

Diana enjoyed the ever popular Margherita pizza. Near a book store that we visited we also were part of the group to see Starbucks open its doors in downtown Helsinki. They have a small store at the Helsinki airport. It is one of those popular world wide icons that you can not escape no matter where you travel!!! Souvenir shops, such as you see in the lower right hand corner, are everywhere.

While we were there in Helsinki we were able to see a major exhibit by a Finnish artist , Tove Jannson,who created an adorable cartoon character during the World War II era called Moomins. Finland is celebrating the centenary of her birth this year, 2014.She was a gifted artist in many mediums but the Moomins, troll like creatures, were her gift to the world. Merchandise connected with these fanciful characters is sold all over the world.Although she has passed, the company set up by she and her brothers to perrpetuate and merchandize the message of her Moomins is located in Helsinki. Tove Jannson is a national treasure for the Finns.

If you are not sure where Finland is located, I would ask you to refer to the globe map at the beginning of the book and see where Tallinn is located. This will help you see where it is geographically in the northern most part of Europe. This will give you a sense of how far north the area is and how cold it can get in the winter.

In downtown Tallinn is a beautiful community theater, the Estonian National Opera house. They publish all plays, musicals and upcoming exhibits on their city webpage so that everyone is informed of events that they might enjoy.It was built in 1913.

It also amazing to see so many wonderful places to eat and enjoy desserts,coffee, tea and certain fast foods.

What trip would be complete without seeing some of America's favorites!!!It always amazes me to see these favorites but they are a more common site than ever. There are also many places which borrow "America" in their restaruant title that make it more appealing to tourists.The food is always great, I sampled a variety of foods by eating out and enjoying the cuisines.

One of my fondest remembrances of Tallinn was seeing ths banner that was downtown hanging over a major street near the downtown park area.

"Life is very hard!" It struck me that it is ironic that this is on the banner. My time in Tallinn was so interesting that it is easy to forget that life has been very hard in this part of our world over the centuries of history. Estonia and its government are working very much toward the goal of changing that banner to "Life used to be very hard!" in my estimation. It is a country with a lot to see and do to help one understand its past history and how that history has been used to bring Estonia into the limelight as a more modern, technologically savvy country for the future.

# Vocabulary

**(These definitions are simplifications of what some key words mean in context)**

1. Diversity – a variety of items

2. Centenary- the hundredth year of an event

3. Technology-the advanced use of computers and related hardware or anything invented to maske man's life easier

4. Medieval-occuring in the 7<sup>th</sup> to the 15<sup>th</sup> centuries, sometimes called the Middle Ages

5. Zenith – at the heighth of success

6. Frieze – a specific art style very popularly used in churches of the Middle Ages; a horizontal band of painting and decoration

7. Marzipan – a popular candy that is pastey and used to create decorative forms

8. Baroque – an ornate style of architecture developed in Europe in the 16<sup>th</sup> century and used until 19<sup>th</sup> century

9. Ornate – decorative with scrolls and curves

# Pronunciations

**(These pronunciations may not be phoenetic in nature but are designated as simple pronnciation guides)**

1. Estonia – S stone ee a

2. Kadriorg – Cad dree org)

3. Tallinn – Towl lean

4. Baroque – baa row k

Printed in the United States
By Bookmasters